Discover and Share

Dinosaurs

Deborah Chancellor

About this book

The **Discover and Share** series enables young readers to read about familiar topics independently. The books are designed to build on children's existing knowledge while providing new information and vocabulary. By sharing this book, either with an adult or another child, young children can learn how to access information, build word recognition skills and develop reading confidence in an enjoyable way.

Reading tips

Begin by finding out what children already know about the topic. Encourage them to talk about it and take the opportunity to introduce vocabulary specific to the topic.

Each image is explained through two levels of text. Confident readers will be able to read the higher level text independently, while emerging readers can try reading the simpler sentences.

Check for understanding of any unfamiliar words and concepts. Inexperienced readers might need you to read some or all of the text to them. Encourage children to retell the information in their own words.

After you have explored the book together, try the quiz on page 22 to see what children can remember and to encourage further discussion.

Contents

Words in **bold** are in the glossary on page 23.

Finding dinosaurs

Huge creatures called dinosaurs roamed the Earth over 65 million years ago.

We know about dinosaurs from their fossils. Fossils are the hard **remains** of animals that lived a very long time ago. Fossils are found in rock.

People dig up fossils to find out more about dinosaurs.

Dinosaurs lived a very long time ago. We find dinosaur fossils in rock.

5

Baby dinosaurs

Dinosaurs were **reptiles.** They laid eggs, just like reptiles do today.

A dinosaur called Maiasaura laid about 30 eggs in her nest.

She looked after her **hatchlings** until they grew big enough to leave the nest.

Dinosaurs laid eggs in nests. Some of them looked after their babies very well.

Gentle giant

Some dinosaurs were enormous. Diplodocus was about 27 metres from head to tail.

That is as long as five elephants standing in a line!

Diplodocus was a **vegetarian**. It used its long neck to reach treetops, or to graze on low plants.

Some dinosaurs were very big. Some were even longer than five elephants standing in a line!

Bone cruncher

This scary dinosaur had very big jaws.

Its teeth were long and sharp.

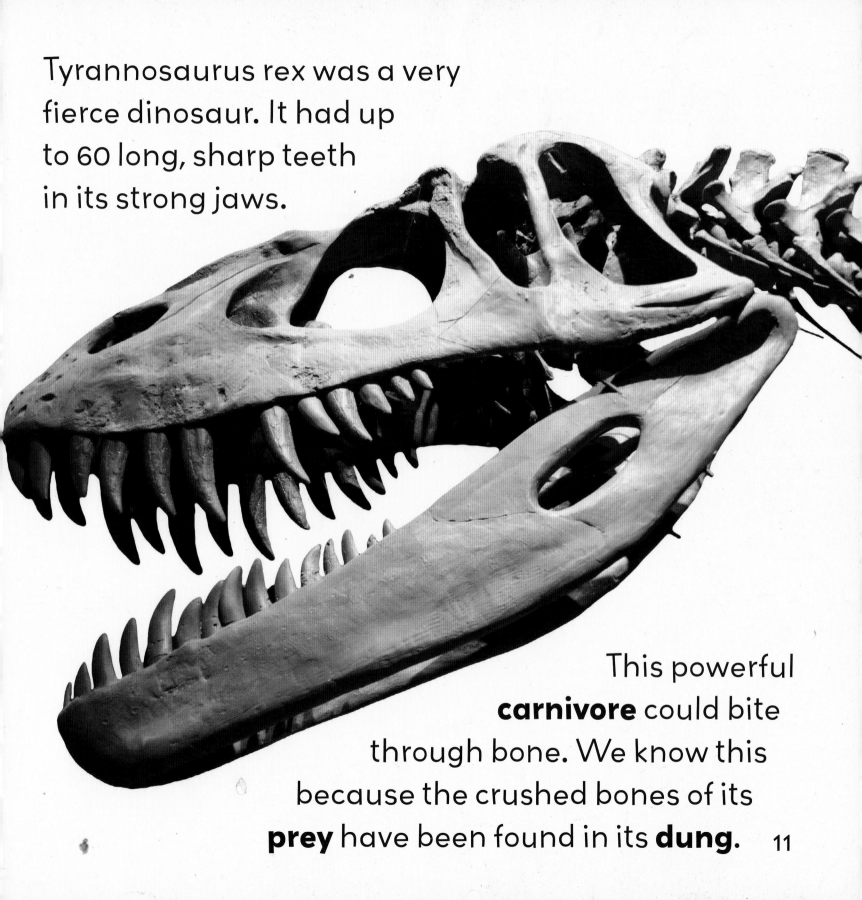

Tyrannosaurus rex was a very fierce dinosaur. It had up to 60 long, sharp teeth in its strong jaws.

This powerful **carnivore** could bite through bone. We know this because the crushed bones of its **prey** have been found in its **dung.**

Fighting machine

Some dinosaurs were good at **defending** themselves from **predators**.

Ankylosaurus had tough **armour** all over its back and sides.

If Ankylosaurus was attacked,
it swung its tail club
at the enemy.

Some dinosaurs had thick body armour.
They were hard to attack.

Quick getaway

Some dinosaurs ran fast on their two back legs. They ran away from other dinosaurs.

For some dinosaurs, running was the only way to escape from danger. Gallimimus ran as fast as a cheetah, at up to 95 kilometres per hour.

Gallimimus' long back legs were built for speed. Its tail helped it to balance during quick turns.

15

Living together

Some dinosaurs lived in groups called herds. There were many dangerous predators around, so it was safer to stick together.

Parasaurolophus used its head **crest** to keep in touch with the herd. The loud honking call it made could be heard from a long way away!

Some dinosaurs lived
in groups called herds.
This helped to keep them safe.

Sea monster

Dinosaurs lived on dry land,
and not in the sea.

The oceans
were full of
many other giant
reptiles, like
Elasmosaurus.

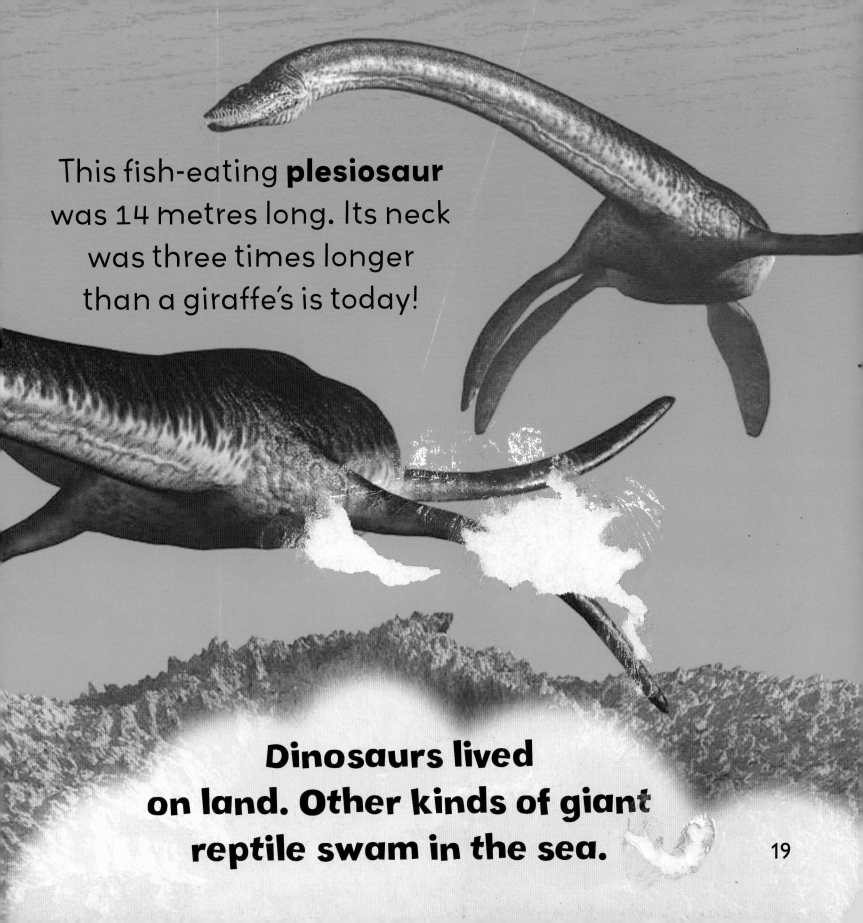

This fish-eating **plesiosaur** was 14 metres long. Its neck was three times longer than a giraffe's is today!

Dinosaurs lived on land. Other kinds of giant reptile swam in the sea.

Early bird

Many **scientists** think a small dinosaur called Archaeopteryx was the first bird.

It had teeth, claws and a bony tail like other dinosaurs, but it also had feathers and wings like a bird. It could probably fly, but not very far or well.

This dinosaur had feathers and wings. It may have been the first bird.

Quiz

1. Where do we find fossils?

2. How many teeth could a Tyrannosaurus Rex have?

3. Why did some dinosaurs have armour?

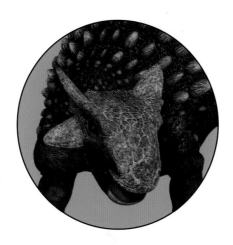

4. Why did some dinosaurs live in herds?

Glossary

armour a tough outer layer that protects an animal
carnivore an animal that only eats meat
crest a ridge of skin or feathers
defend to keep safe
dung animal poo
hatchling an animal that has hatched from an egg
plesiosaur a long-necked sea reptile
predator an animal that hunts other animals
prey an animal that is hunted by other animals
remains the parts of something that are left behind
   when the rest has disappeared
reptile a scaly animal that lays eggs
scientist someone who finds out about the world
vegetarian an animal that only eats plants

Answers to the quiz:
1. In rock.
2. Up to 60.
3. To protect themselves from attack.
4. To keep safe from predators.

Index

Franklin Watts
Published in Great Britain in 2017 by
The Watts Publishing Group

Copyright ©The Watts Publishing
Group 2015

Series Editor: Julia Bird
Series Advisor: Karina Law
Series Design: Basement68

Every attempt has been made to clear
copyright. Should there be any
inadvertent omission please apply to
the publisher for rectification.

Dewey number: 567.9
ISBN 978 1 4451 3803 9

Franklin Watts
An imprint of
Hachette Children's Group
Part of The Watts Publishing Group
Carmelite House
50 Victoria Embankment
London EC4Y 0DZ

An Hachette UK Company

www.hachette.co.uk
www.franklinwatts.co.uk

MIX
Paper from
responsible sources
FSC® C104740
www.fsc.org

These are the lists of contents for each title in *Discover and Share*:

Animal Homes

Safe shelter • Snowy home • Underground town • Tall tower • Dark cave • Rocky rest • Grassy nest • Hermit home • Fishy shelter • Quiz • Glossary and answers • Index

Bugs

... bug? • Hungry bug • I am a ... • Flying bug • Hidden hunter • ...s • Jumping bugs • Bug home • ... bugs • Quiz • Glossary • Index

...Road

...ces • Pedal power • Hot wheels • ... • Speed racer • Off to work • Big ... On the buses • City tram • Quiz • ... • Index

... pet? • Looking after a pet • ... dogs • Cool cats • Rabbits in the ... Hamster home • Hungry lizards ...nk • Visiting the vet • Quiz • Glossary • Index

Seaside

What is the seaside? • Changing tides • Building sandcastles • Sea shells • Crafty crabs • Rock pool • Going fishing • The harbour • Sea breeze • Quiz • Glossary • Index

Seasons

What are the seasons? • Winter trees • Spring lambs • Chicks • Summer flowers • Hot sunshine • Autumn fruit • Falling leaves • Ready for winter • Quiz • Glossary • Index

Dinosaurs

Finding dinosaurs • Baby dinosaurs • Gentle giant • Bone cruncher • Fighting machine • Quick getaway • Living together • Sea monster • Early bird • Quiz • Glossary and answers • Index

Planet Earth

Blue planet • Frozen zones • Dry deserts • Rainforests • Coral reefs • Mountains • Running rivers • Grasslands • Where we live • Quiz • Glossary • Index

Human Body

Amazing body • Super skeleton • On the move • Pumping power • Hard work • Eat for energy • Control centre • Making sense • Keeping well • Quiz • Glossary and answers • Index

Space

Where is space? • Sunny days • The Moon • Amazing planets • Endless stars • Blast off! • Inside a spacecraft • On the Moon • Exploring Mars • Quiz • Glossary and answers • Index

Reading Level Guidance
Book Band: 7 Turquoise

Discover and Share

DINOSAURS

The mighty dinosaurs ruled Earth millions of years ago. Find out all about them, from peaceful plant-eaters to fierce carnivores.

Discover the facts and **Share** the learning in these fun books with text written at two levels. The higher level text is perfect for more confident readers. Alongside it, a simpler text contains the key facts. This means that readers of a range of abilities can read, share and enjoy together.

The text has been checked by Karina Law, a former teacher, who is now a literacy consultant and writer.

Titles in the series:

978 1 4451 3646 2

978 1 4451 3591 5

978 1 4451 3803 9

978 1 4451 3797 1

978 1 4451 3648 6

978 1 4451 3647 9

978 1 4451 3807 7

978 1 4451 3655 4

978 1 4451 3590 8

978 1 4451 3810 7

Download free activity sheets at www.franklinwatts.co.uk

FRANKLIN WATTS

FSC®

£7.99

ISBN 978-1-4451-3803-9

9 781445 138039

www.franklinwatts.co.uk